Yes I Am Human I Know You Were Wondering

Erin Dorney

Autofocus Books
Easton, PA | Orlando, FL

Published by Autofocus Books
autofocusbooks.com

1st printing

LC Genre/Form Terms: *Epistolary poetry.* | *Visual poetry.* | *Collages.* | *Found poetry.* | *Prose poems.* | *Parasocial relationships--Poetry.*

ISBN 978-1-957392-36-3 (paperback; acid-free paper)
LCCN 2024944234 (print)

Cover design by Amy Wheaton

Yes I Am Human
I Know You Were
Wondering

Italicized text indicates found phrases from
Adriene Mishler's *Yoga with Adriene* YouTube channel.

TABLE OF CONTENTS

Day 1....................9
Day 2....................11
Day 3....................13
Day 4....................15
Day 5....................17
Day 6....................18
Day 7....................20
Day 8....................23
Day 9....................25
Day 10....................27
Day 11....................29
Day 12....................31
Day 13....................32
Day 14....................34
Day 15....................36
Day 16....................41
Day 17....................43
Day 18....................45
Day 19....................47
Day 20....................49
Day 21....................50
Day 22....................52
Day 23....................55
Day 24....................57
Day 25....................59
Day 26....................61
Day 27....................62
Day 28....................65
Day 29....................66
Day 30....................68

it was so long since I had eaten green leaves

I felt myself becoming a plant again

—Colette

DAY 1

Dear Adriene,

When you said *ground down* I thought you said brown down, like beef, because just before that you mentioned the *nutrients of your practice*—each day I do, practice, drop another effervescent tablet in the jam jar on the sink. I watch a mother watch her daughter read about her hair and consider all the other moms I'm missing. Outside, babies grow and I facilitate it from the concrete patio. I can't decide which body part to use as the thread that stitches me through time and space, what have you got for that? *Just begin to arrive.* Why do I feel proud standing beneath a tall chestnut tree when I have stood under so many before without feeling any pride at all? Dirt around my fingernails like a silk dress. Tissue on a black shirt through the wash. One day we will all be it—I could be holding handfuls of you now.

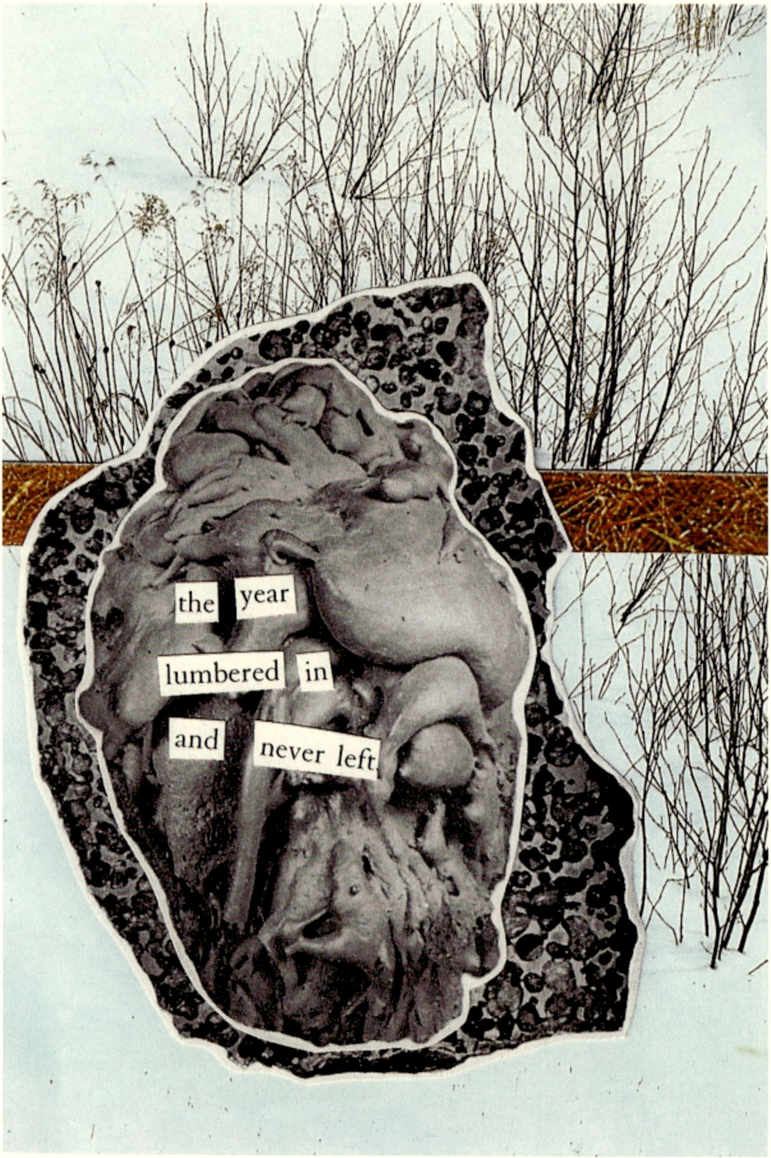
the year
lumbered in
and never left

DAY 2

Dear Adriene,

When I was home I thought about what you'd said—*fold in towards it.* Some unabashed pride, some handsome lawn. Like how weeds are simply plants in the wrong place. Summer's drying out, just flit and rot like bachelor's buttons, featherfew for migraines. *What does your heart say? What do you want to return to?* I fell right down in the yard, foot in a hole, and spotted someone through the fence. Have you seen a bird that's half red and half white underneath? Because I have. *The breath always comes first*—except when it doesn't.

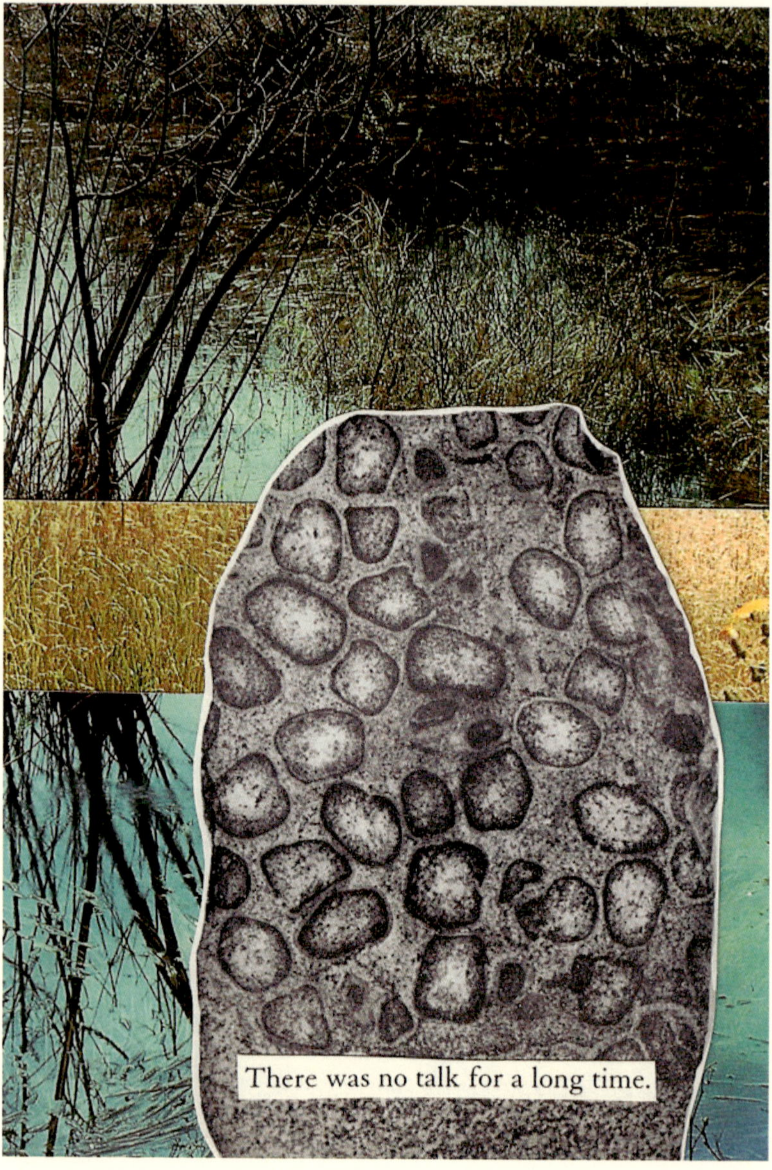
There was no talk for a long time.

DAY 3

Dear Adriene,

I'll tell you a secret—water brings me things. Did you know that glass can take one hundred years to weather? Each wave a rock, pebble tumbled soft, fossil at my feet. You say, *claw through the hands*, so I do, each morning desperate to see if a piece of the moon has finally come. When it rains the garden garbage rises—undead. Rusted nails, broken bulbs, a button, one cent, they reverse-sift themselves up into my palms. *Fingertips kiss the earth*, as I drag trash away from whatever good is growing. Lately I've licked so many things off leaves—a globe of pollen, a bead of wetness in which I saw the world. *Make a choice.*

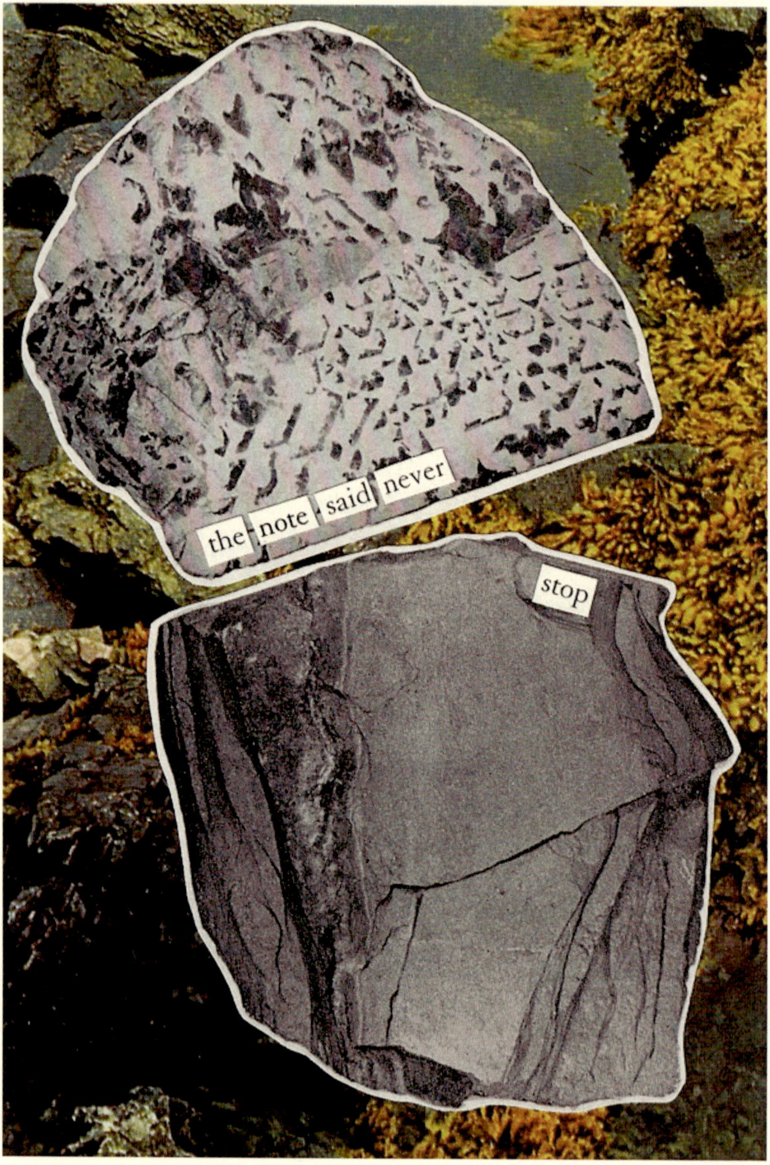
the note said never
stop

DAY 4

Dear Adriene,

I carried it on my tongue to different parts of the yard like some bee. All day I felt it in the back of my throat, a whistle. My dog will eat anything I hand him, but he won't take this from my lips. *I call this smoothing the heart forward.* I call this an informal survey. I only listen to the radio when it arrives in languages I do not understand. I saw a limp seagull vomit, tangled in seaweed, and you weren't even there. Falling on its face like a deadrise, just another useless knot. *Let gravity do the work.* Did you know most pollen carries a small amount of electrostatic charge? I feel it on my brow, my lips, between the small hairs packed closely together on my legs.

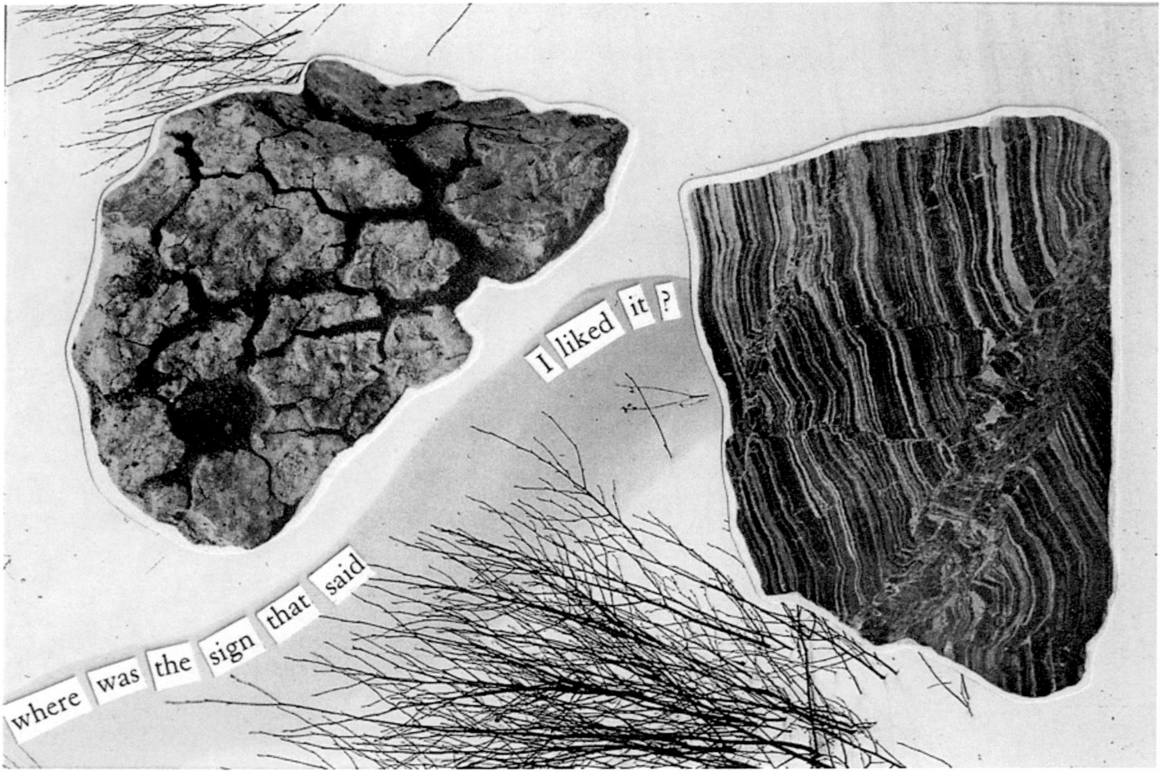
where was the sign that said
I liked it ?

DAY 5

Dear Adriene,

How does it feel? I love when I can pick you fast with both hands.

DAY 6

Dear Adriene,

It has been six days since my last letter, six days since I severed the sunflower's head too soon. Its green tube turned black today—the whole plant melted before my eyes. Last week I dreamt a cat had kittens but one runt was just an unfurled flower bud. *Move like you love yourself.* But what if I don't? What if I never have? A wave of crushed cattails crashes into summer creek beds where the white-tailed deer lie down. *Relax away the body completely into the earth.*

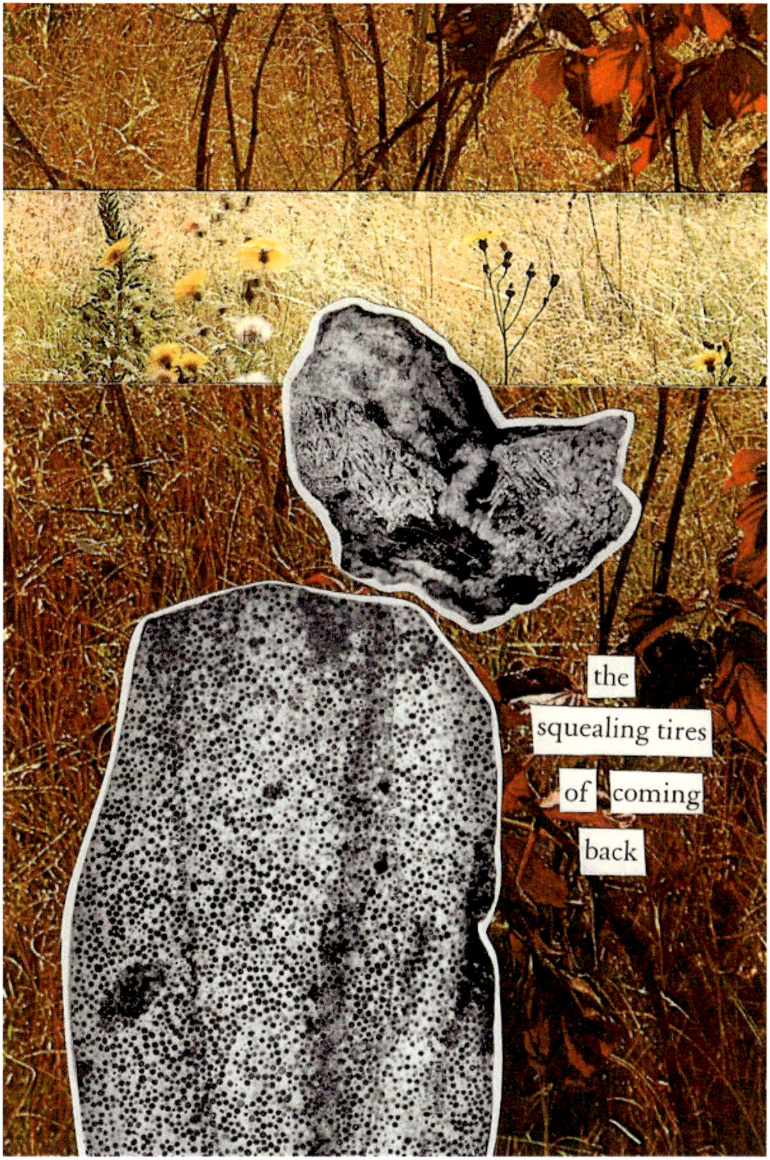
the
squealing tires
of coming
back

DAY 7

Dear Adriene,

Just a loving scan. I will not Google you.

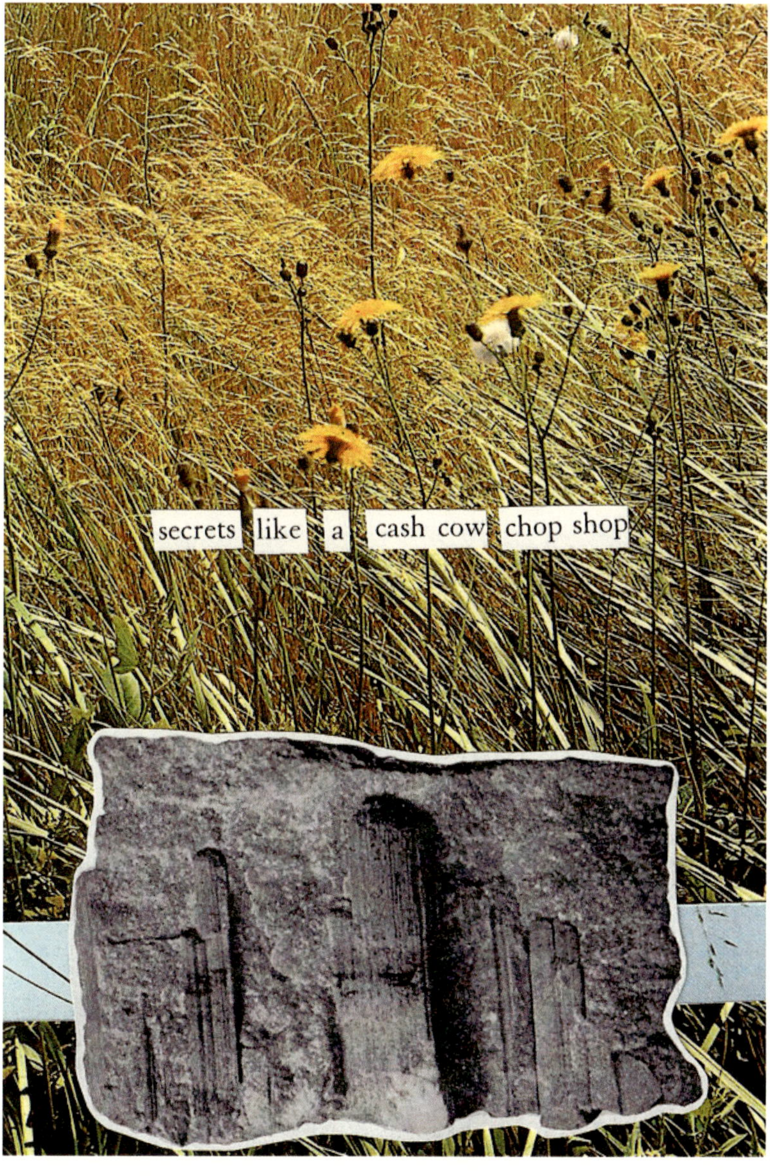
secrets like a cash cow chop shop

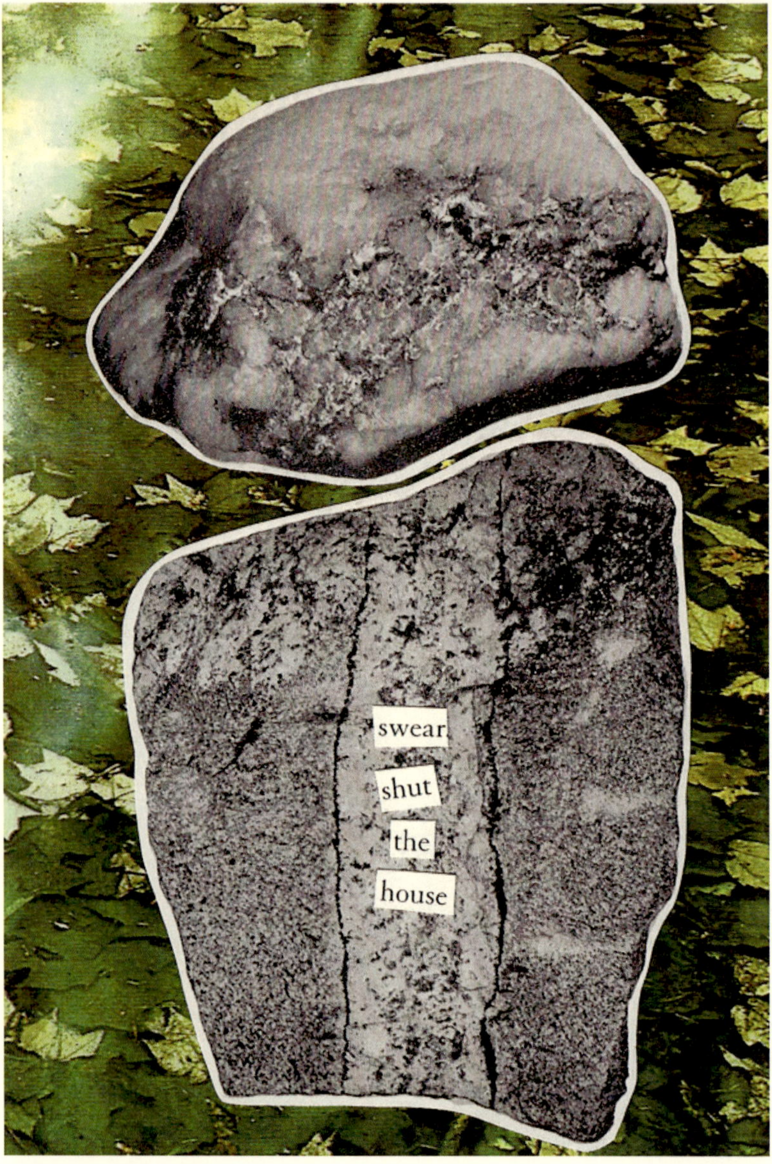
swear
shut
the
house

DAY 8

Dear Adriene,

Carve a line with your nose—just one more way to hollow out. I don't miss driving past the landfill, its scent of something seriously wrong. *Where the attention goes, the energy flows*, but then why do we bury our trash or shoot it out into space? I wish just once a leaf would grow large enough to wrap me like a blanket, but they're always disappointing. Like the squash vine by midday, wilted in the heat, then a million begging hands by sunrise. My eyes are like two old coins, rubbed fuzzy in a nervous pocket. What is worth seeing now? Name me one thing that hasn't let you down.

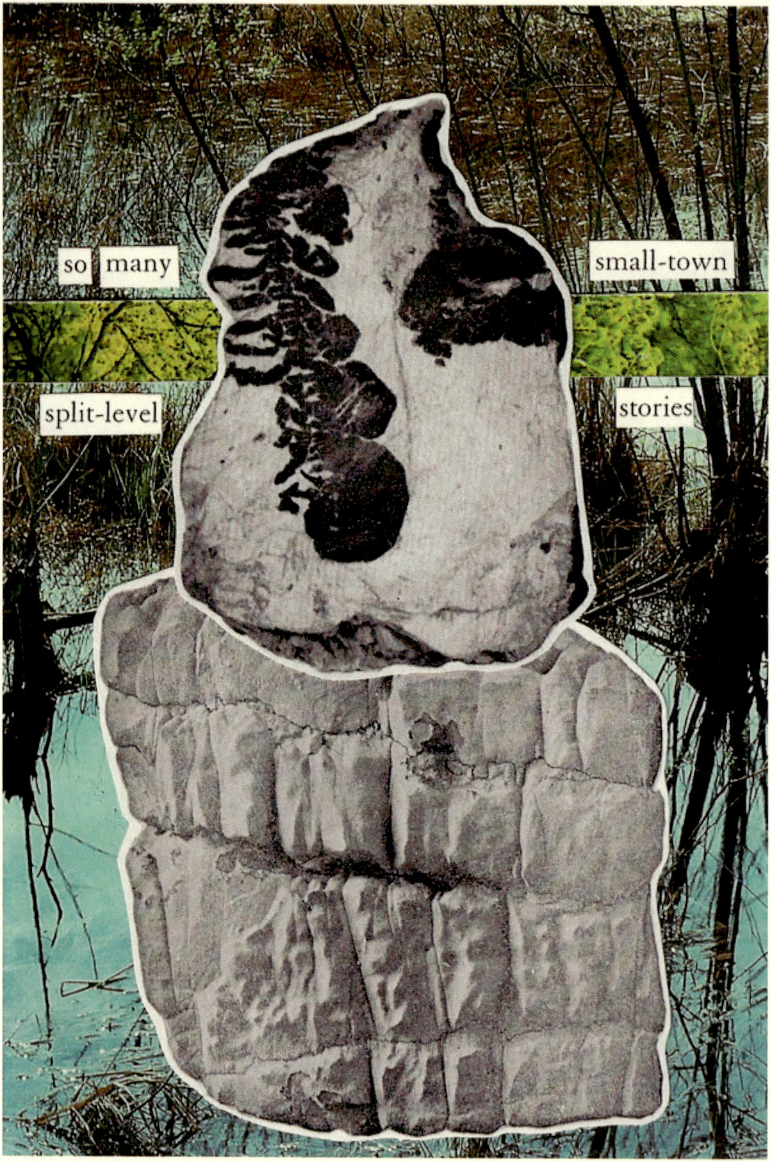
so many
small-town
split-level
stories

DAY 9

Dear Adriene,

The planthoppers lay an average of forty eggs at once. Does that mean they live for one year or forty one? Eighty two? One hundred and twenty three? *Allow that information to travel*— in swarms, let it rain down like a plague. It doesn't seem fair. Quarantine came first for the lanternflies and then it came for us, our grapes, our apples, hops, and hardwoods. Everything I think is a black block outlined in grey—reticulated. What's being done is nothing. *Imagine yourself as a baby.* Now imagine a whole country of that.

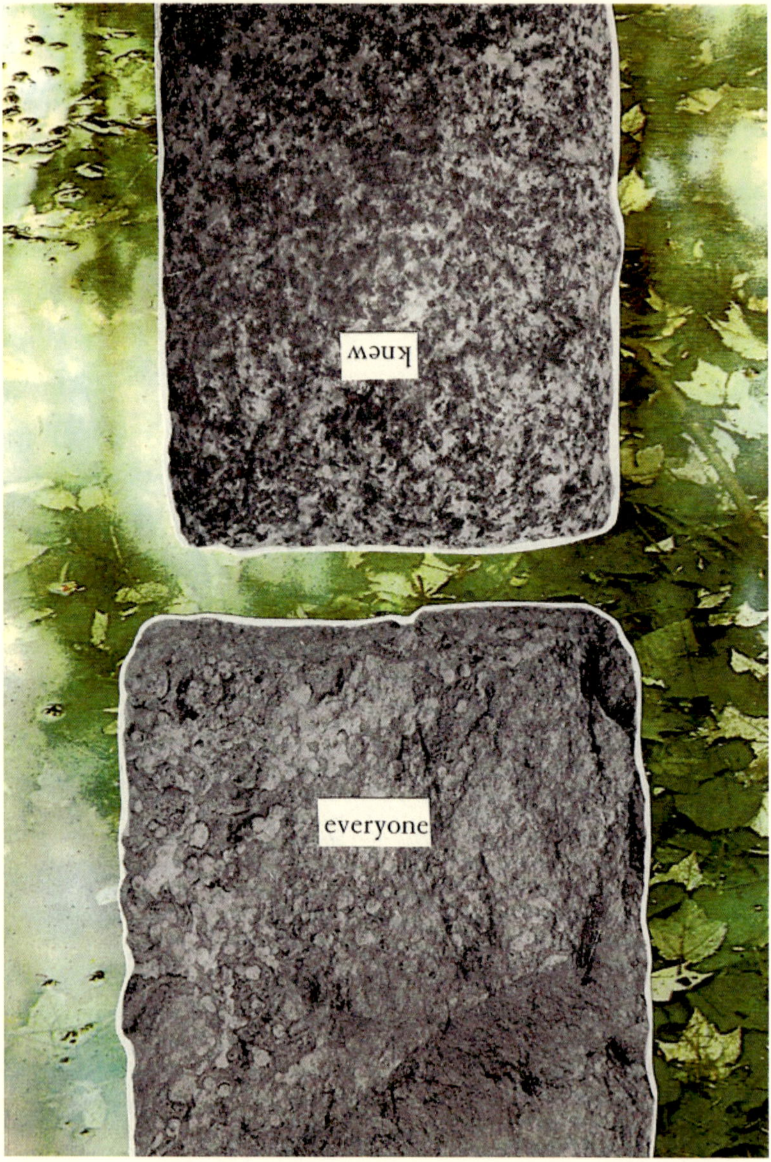
knew
everyone

DAY 10

Dear Adriene,

Every virtue signaled. Every lawn-boy. Every lady holding a platter with outstretched arms. Every nightfall, every windbreak, every morning tumbling wet. Every petal dropped, every dropped signal, every time anyone even thought to ask. I think: sunshine as punishment, lavender as love language, how some of our insides hold dead things and we don't even know it. *Shine a little light into those dark crevices of the body.* A grain silo can be a metaphor for any feeling—one misstep and you are simply engulfed. Did you know suffocation rarely occurs from the weight of it? It is the grain itself that kills you, filling your every inch of throat.

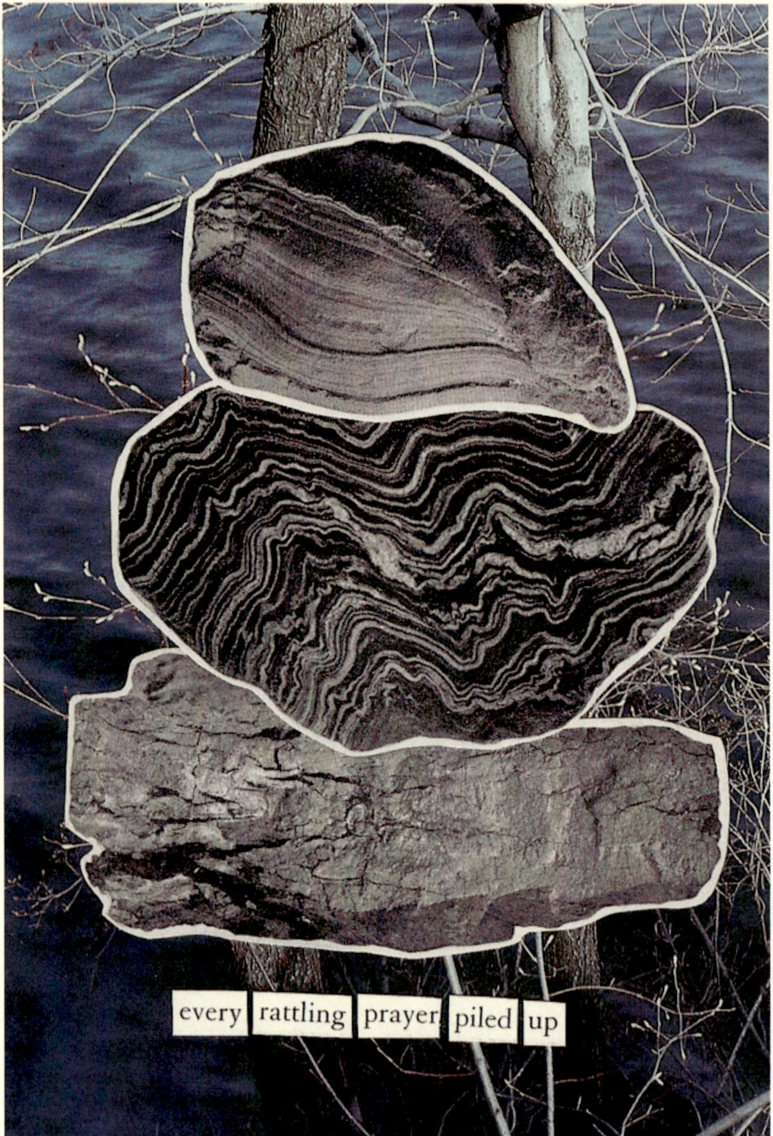
every rattling prayer piled up

DAY 11

Dear Adriene,

How about the feeling when you've confidently identified a flower and years later find out you're wrong? *Super important not to collapse here.* And if you discovered a brand new sound, how would you know for sure? There are at least six boards that can be cut from a single tree for boat building—you push the whole thing through the chewer like Play-Doh shooting out in squiggles. To burn the wood's the only way to smush it back together. *Just notice the bones,* you said, but mine have never broken. For all I know they're gnawed off at the ends. Is a beaver dam a tool? There's some contention here. I myself have never trusted footing on wet wood, the slow slide into cool water. Imagine coming across your own bones on a footpath through the woods, screaming white against the moss.

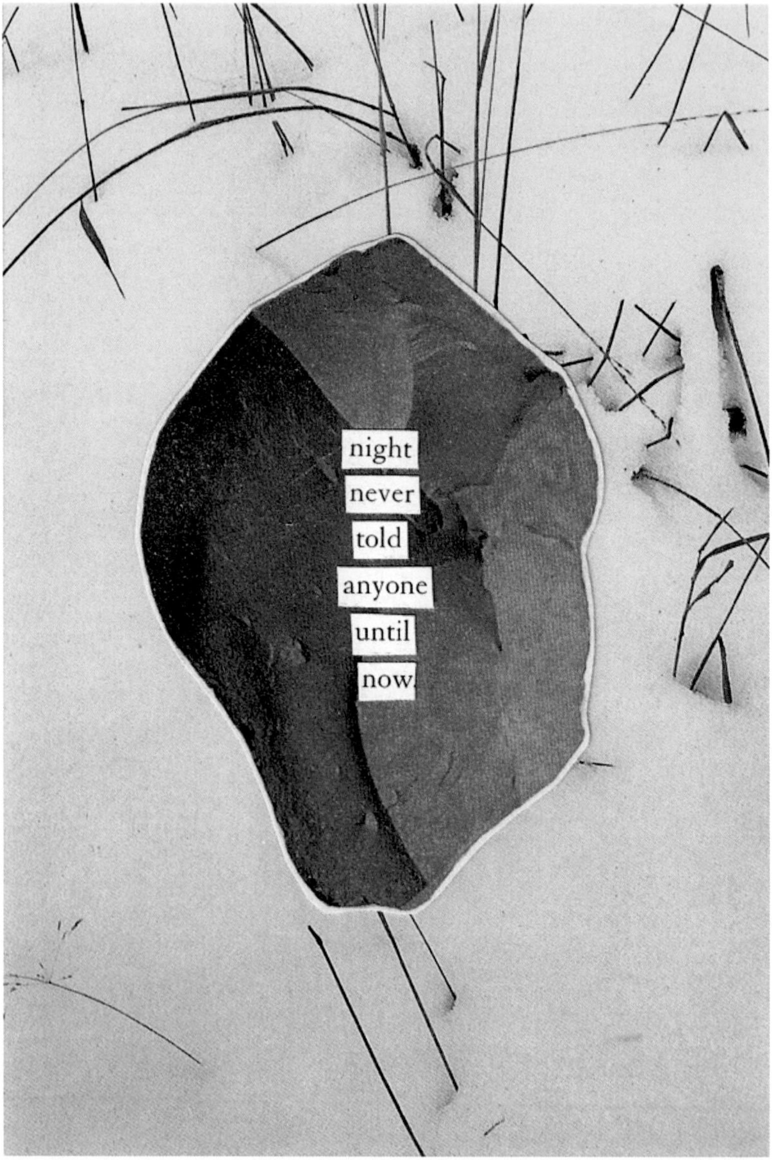
night
never
told
anyone
until
now.

DAY 12

Dear Adriene,

My body is a list of things I'm still figuring out. *Energetically.* Like white roots worming out of brown seeds on top of wet soil. On my stoop I gave away hundreds of plants but still had to throw some away. Was I born in one piece, or many that have come together over time? When two houseplants grow to touch each other, how can that not be intentional? *A fun little dance with gravity.*

DAY 13

Dear Adriene,

Travel up and down the spine—long belly. I keep telling myself I'll do more when this is over, but what if it never ends? Is your mouth different or have you just grown in around your teeth? Your voice changes, but I don't know how many years it's been. One thing I know for sure—over time your background empties out. Men move dirt (as they always have) and I watch as a place where I've stood is buried under two tons of rock. There are always two stories, two gull wings attached to no body. When I drove eighty down the backroads of my hometown, a turkey vulture in the other lane never flinched. *Take a couple quiet breaths.*

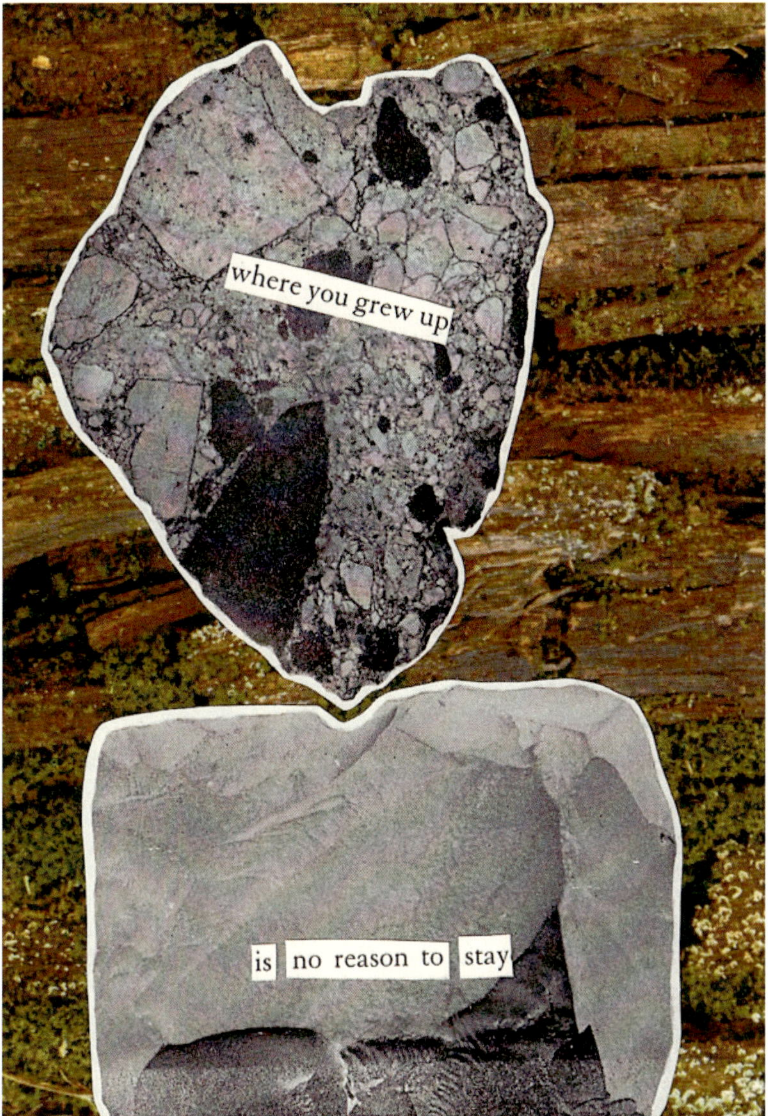
where you grew up
is no reason to stay

DAY 14

Dear Adriene,

There are so many people doing this with you right now. This brings me as much comfort as finding a stag head mounted on a magnificent stone hearth with its tongue dangling out. We are the taxidermied trying to twist. Like, okay, I'm not alone, but now I am suspicious. *I can't control anything anyway. I can only control how I move.* My mat reeks of jealousy, and still, I make plans to meet you again tomorrow.

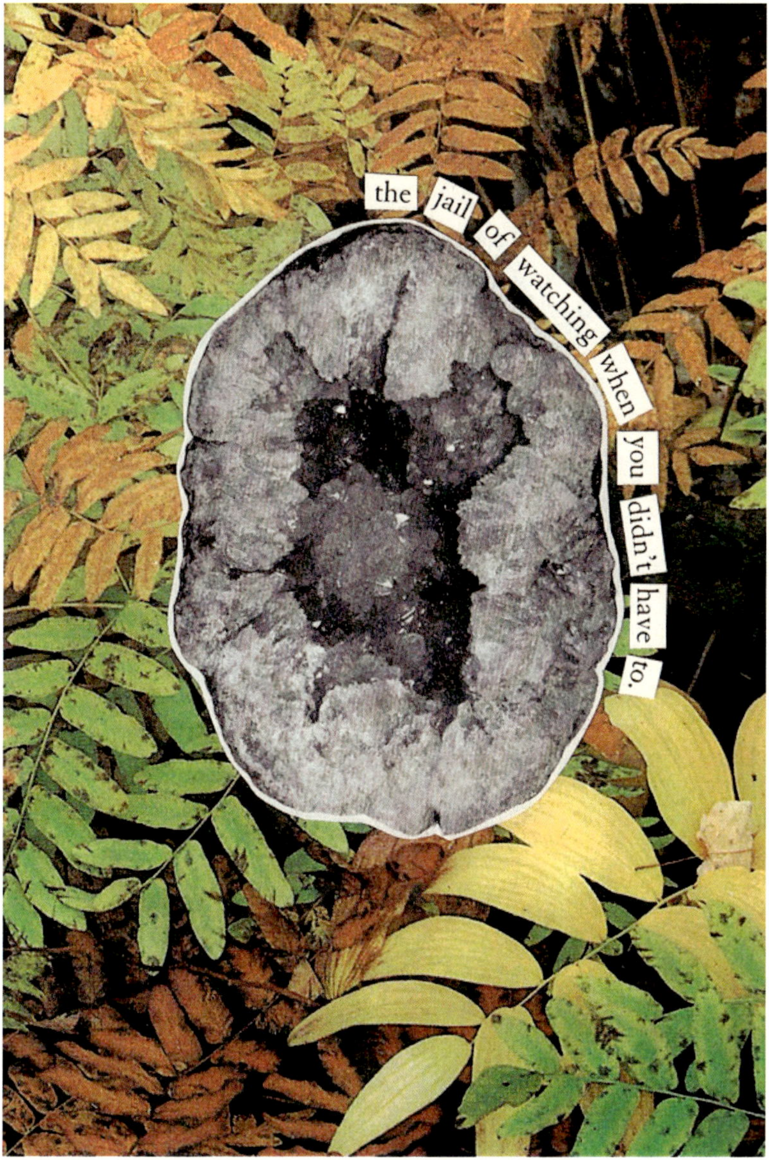
the jail of watching when you didn't have to.

DAY 15

Dear Adriene,

Is it steady?
Is it cracked?
Imagine the stick
as the spine.

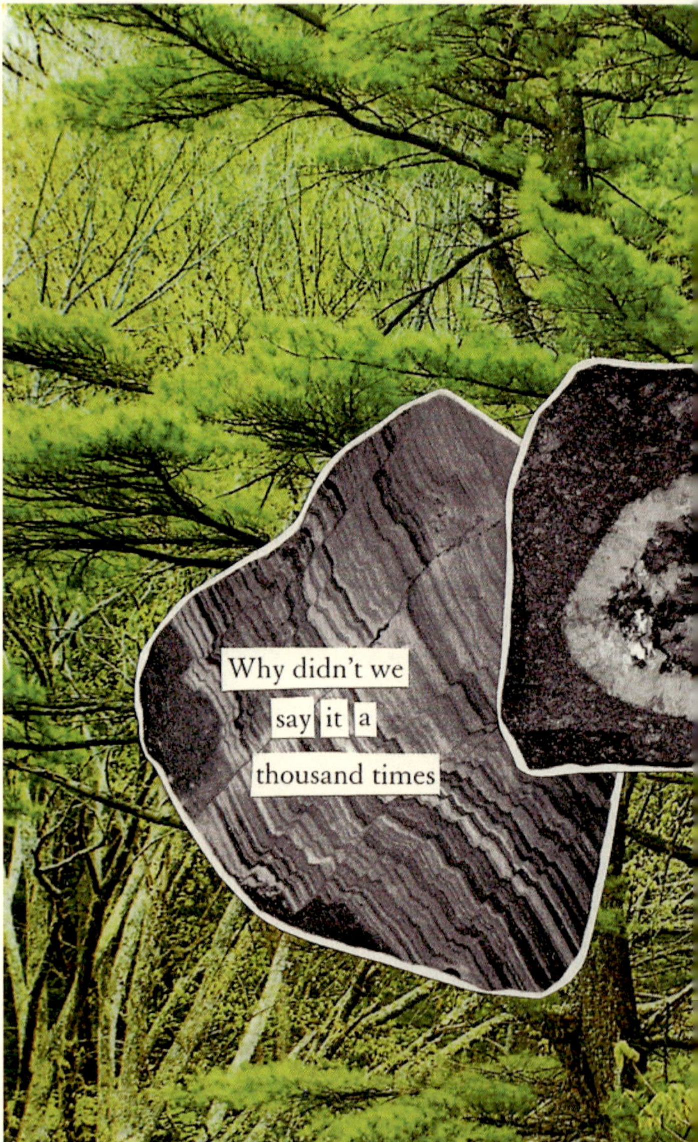
Why didn't we
say it a
thousand times

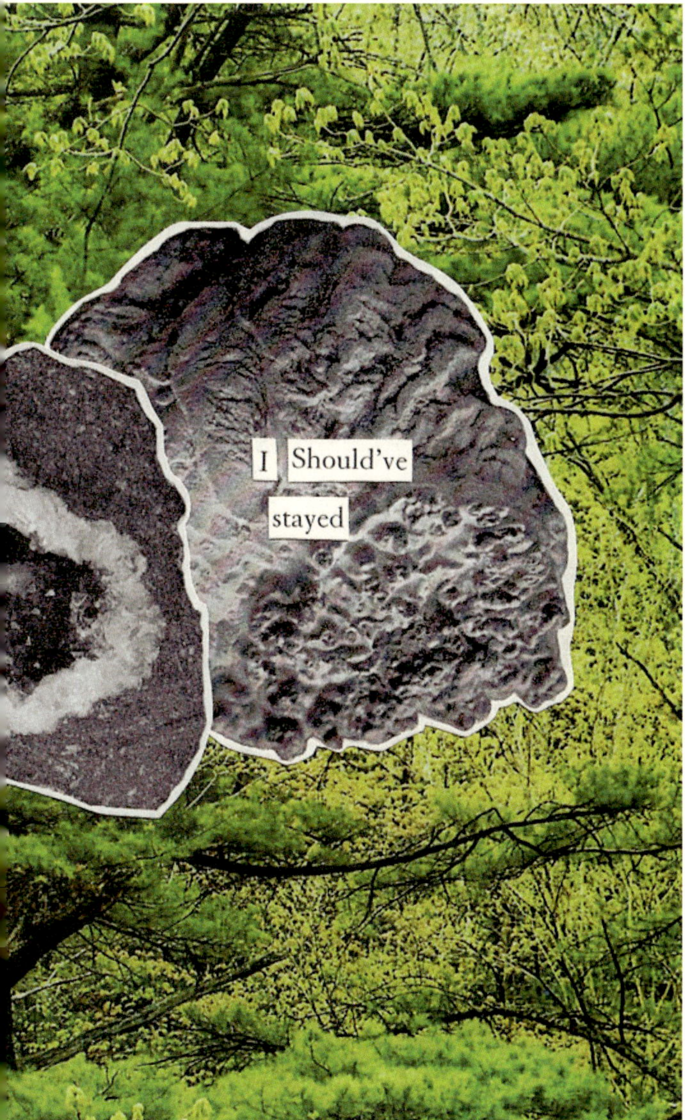
I Should've
stayed

DAY 16

Dear Adriene,

For sixteen days I watch you watch me, but you never see me in the basement, next to the dog puke stain, outside the laundry room, the attic. Sometimes there is no sun and I lie down on a bed of dirt. *We're almost done.* Where will you go when this is all over? To the next room for a sandwich? To stand barefoot in front of the fridge? *This is where we're gonna end it today.* I saw the reflection of studio lights in the window behind your body, warped like cardboard left out in the rain. They say I could pay money to be in the same room as you. I'd rather sink my forehead to the ground—breathe you into the soft coiled curve of each foot.

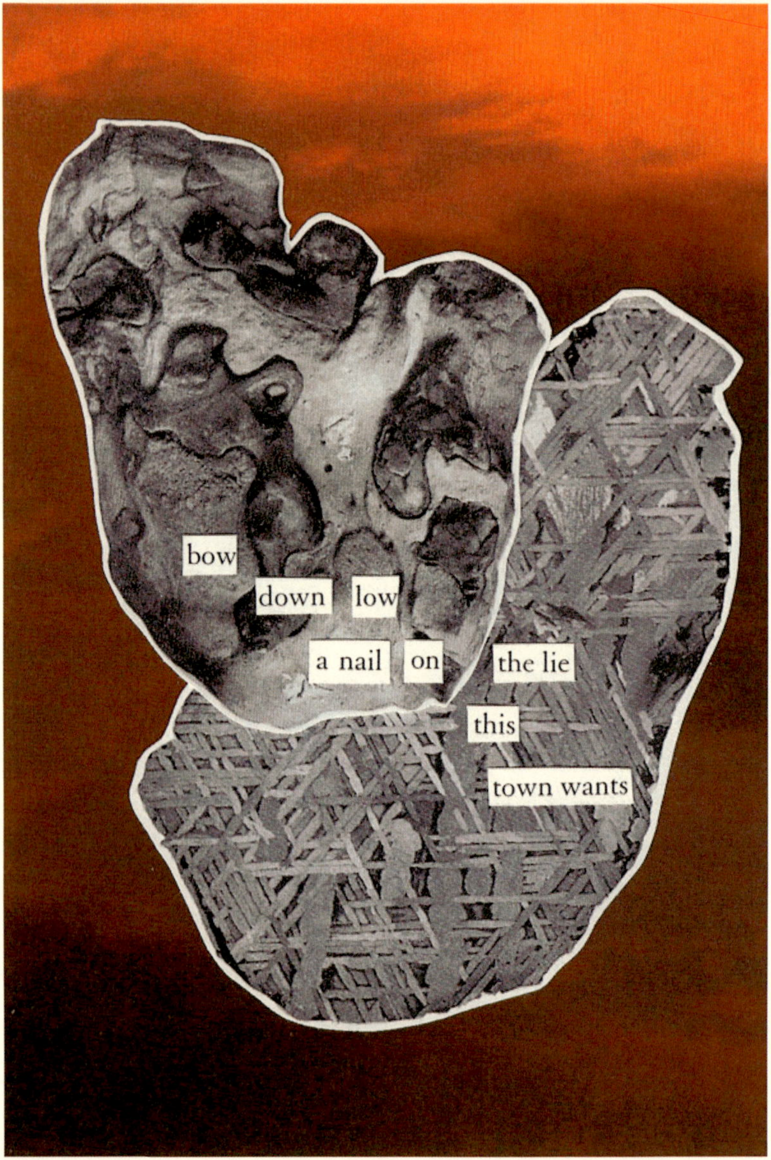
bow
down low
a nail on
the lie
this
town wants

DAY 17

Dear Adriene,

Imagine someone softly kissing you on the neck here. Don't worry about who's kissing you. I worry. *What's going on with your face? What's going on with your breath?*

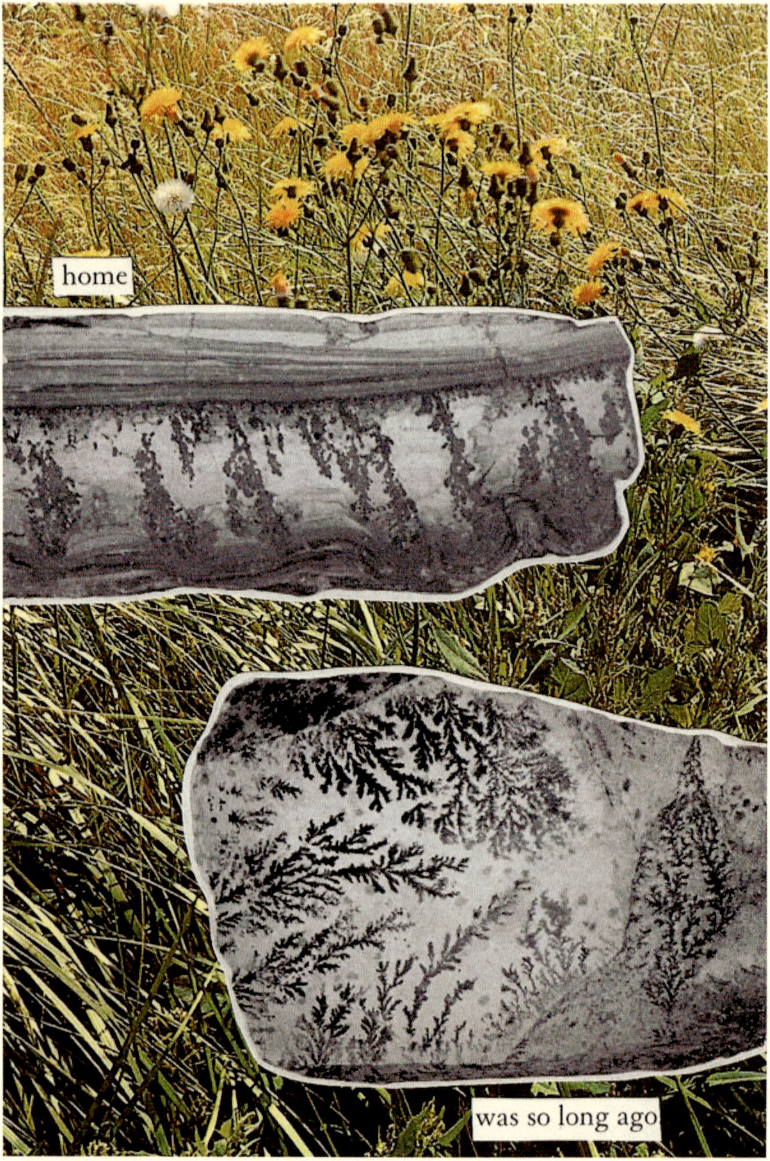
home
was so long ago

DAY 18

Dear Adriene,

Imagine waking after a surgery and not knowing how many holes your body has. That the number could change over the course of your living. *Pretend like you're hearing good news.* I gasp each time I notice what they've done to trees around power lines. Today I had to look at the sky for so long, just to get all the other pictures out of my head.

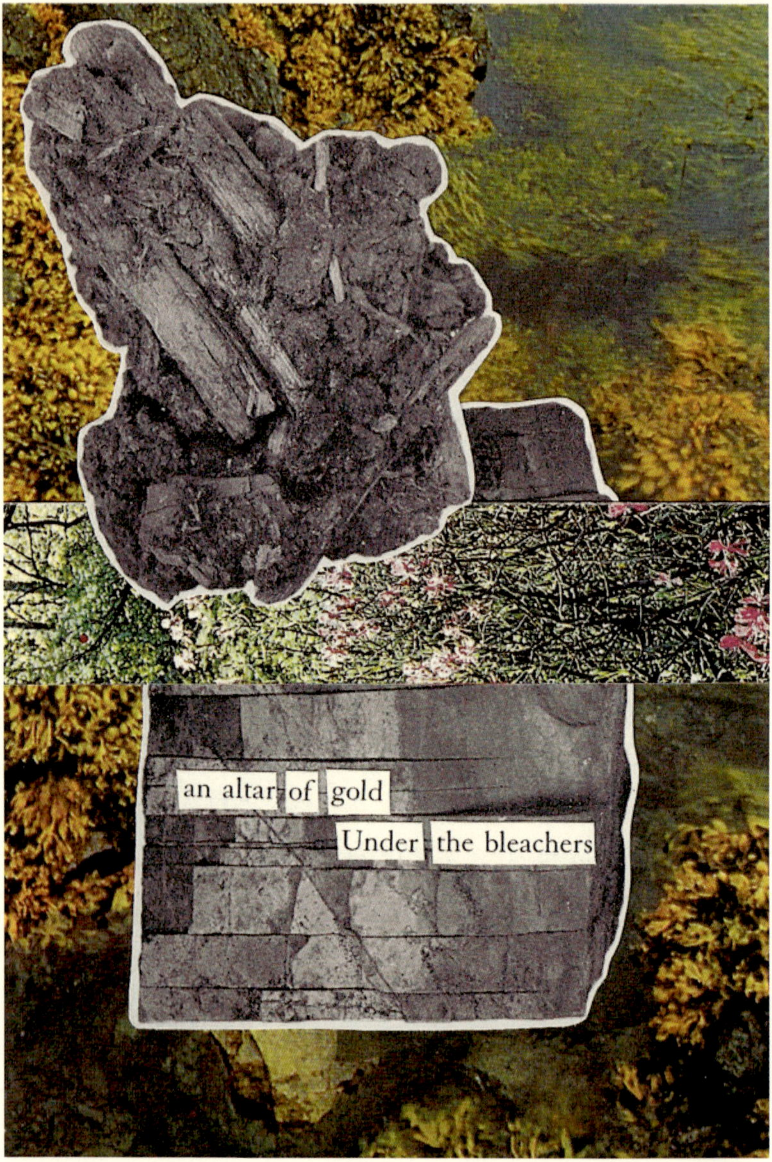
an altar of gold
Under the bleachers

DAY 19

Dear Adriene,

Did you know you can't see space but you can see objects in it? *In the jaw. I'm not putting on a disguise or hiding.* It's a fact that I can't forget your face. Imagine being the first person to walk on the moon but never bending down to touch it. The suits don't move that way. *Feel supported by the earth.* Outside is a loon's long wail, night chorusing while we sleep. They say in space there's noise, but not the kind any human can hear.

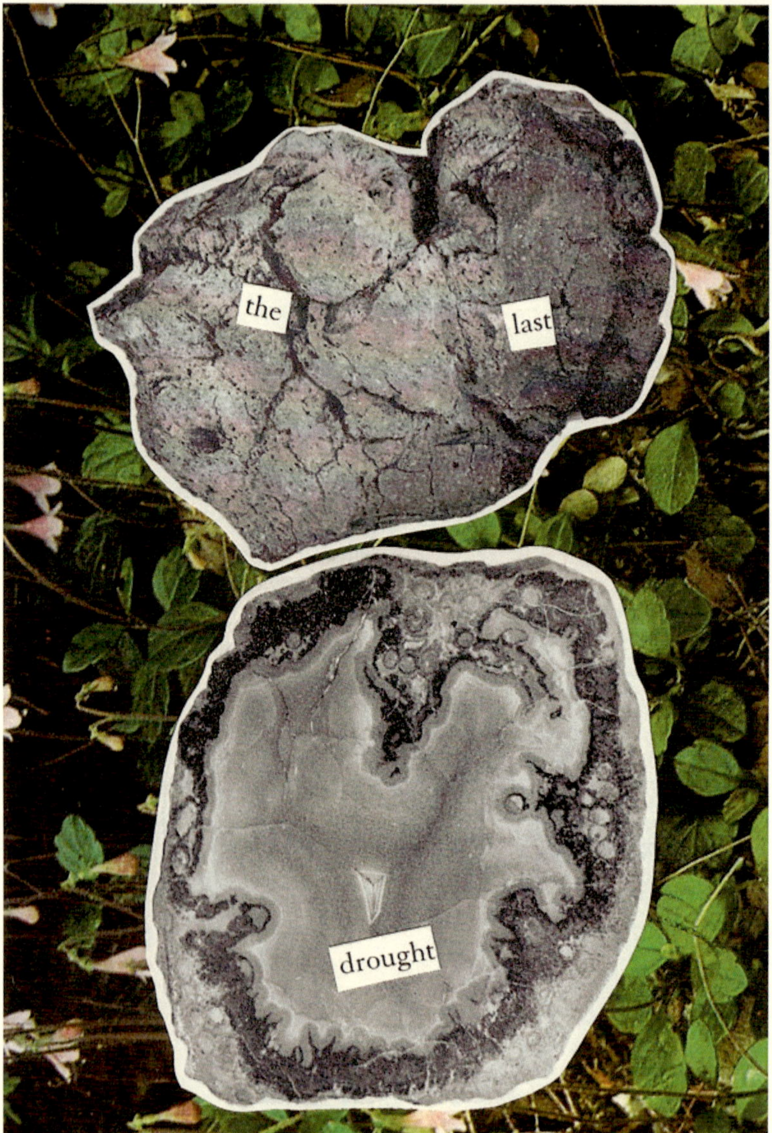
the
last
drought

DAY 20

Dear Adriene,

What's bad for me is good for you—tension, stress, that whinge in my shoulders. I sit at home and you welcome it. What does it feel like to have everyone tune you in? I watch a tick climb until I lose track of it, like time. Each day recirculates. *The system is go.* It breaks down every twenty minutes. Milkweed to seed and some wrinkled fern. I watch myself watch you and hate every second of the sensation.

DAY 21

Dear Adriene,

Teach me how to talk to invisible things. How to measure shoreline length. *Focus on a steady state.* How can some things twist in my mind like morning glories? I think I am invasive. I keep saying no but you grow into all my empty spaces. *Dear ones*, how you multiply.

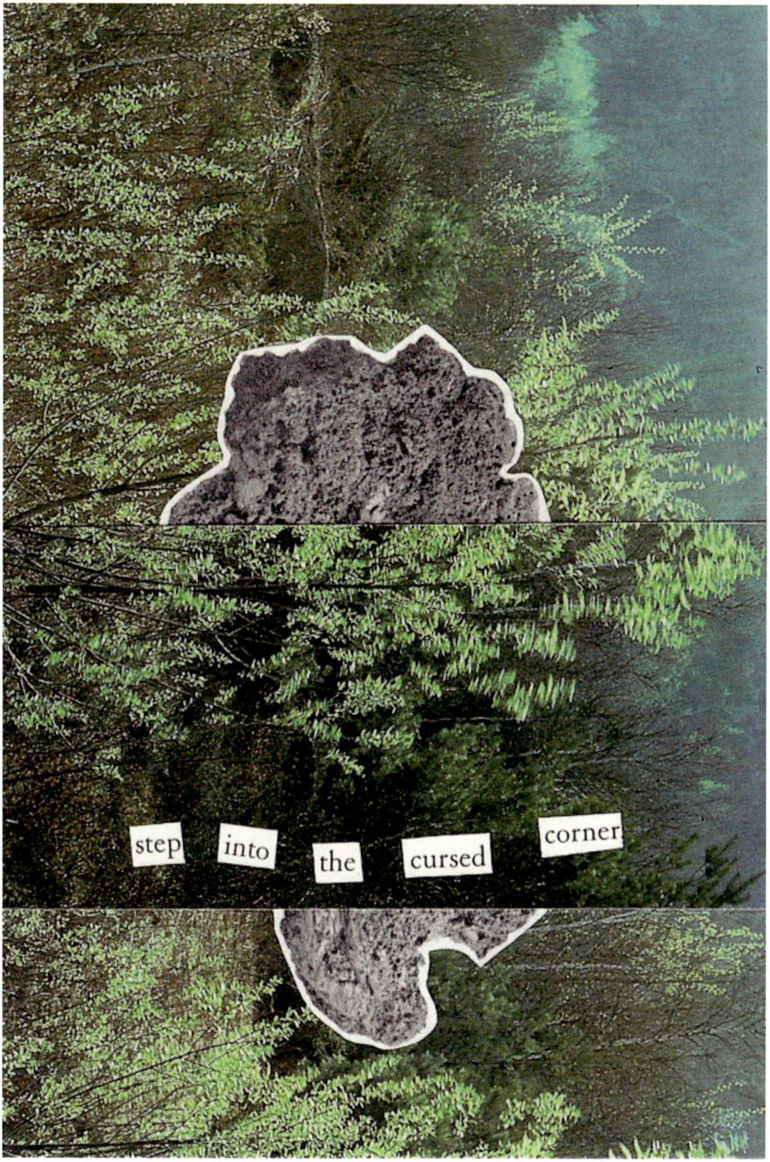
step into the cursed corner

DAY 22

Dear Adriene,

This time is for you—each morning crusted eyelid, each knee pressed down on mouse shit, curve toward carpet my fingers cringe at. How will we choose to spend these days we have left? You say *be there fully* but you never say where—and I have tried so many spots. A place can disappear right before your eyes, through an email, through a text. I try to make a third, new thing—between what was, what I remember, and what is—but everything is piecemeal. Everything is roughshod. *Allow release & let go.*

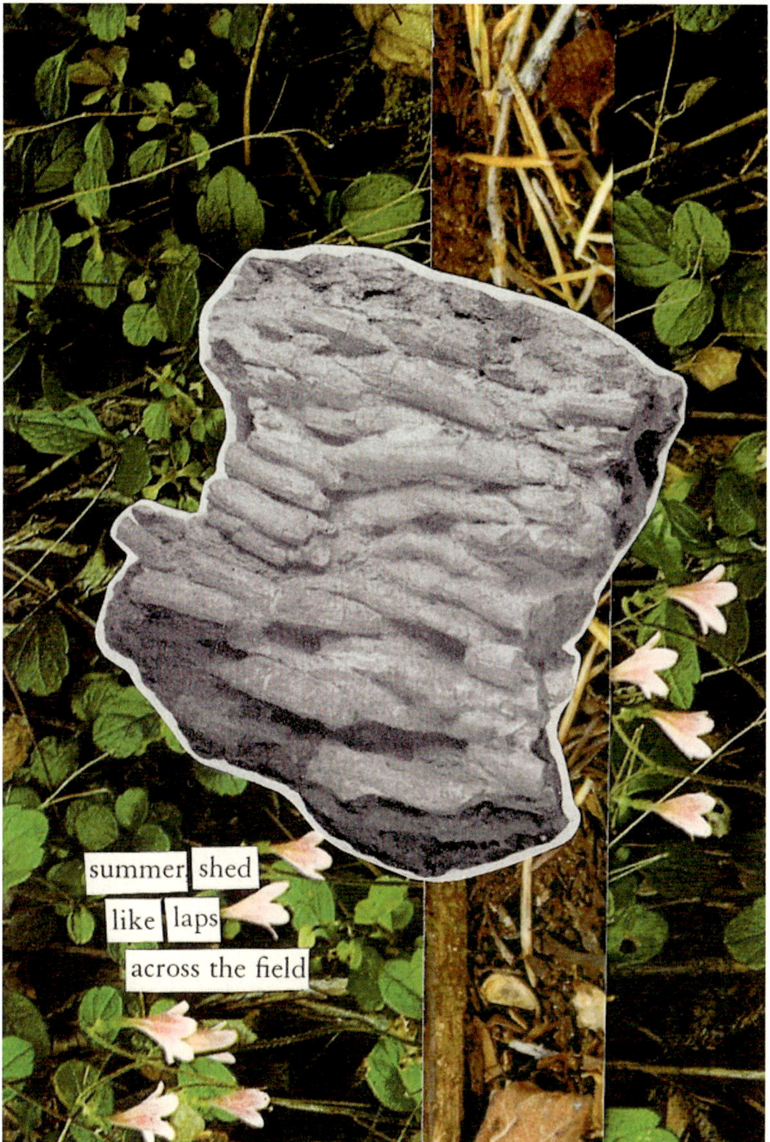
summer shed
like laps
across the field

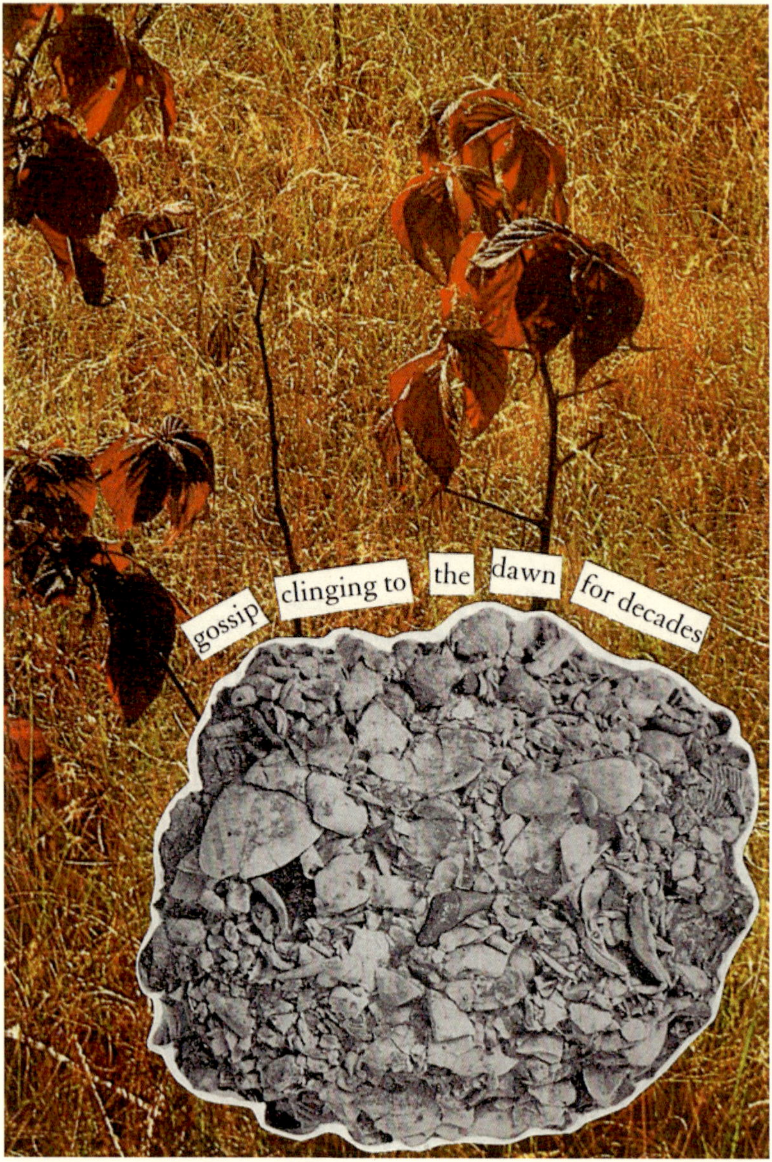
gossip
clinging to
the
dawn
for decades

DAY 23

Dear Adriene,

Women are a fluctuation, a scent gone cold. We are things made out of other things. Imagine yourself as a chandelier made of deer antlers; a lamp handcrafted from an old gun. There are mountains that keep on rising, almost a foot per hundred years, and this gives me hope. *We all need some support.* Quit the past and it becomes obvious, like time fringing another pocket. I would have told about the way water rushes into radiator pipes, whooshing, how I heard an honest-to-god tree fall in the forest, crashing. *Sounds are welcome in this practice.* How can there be so many different shades of green? *Sweet sip of air.* I'll keep trying to find you in them.

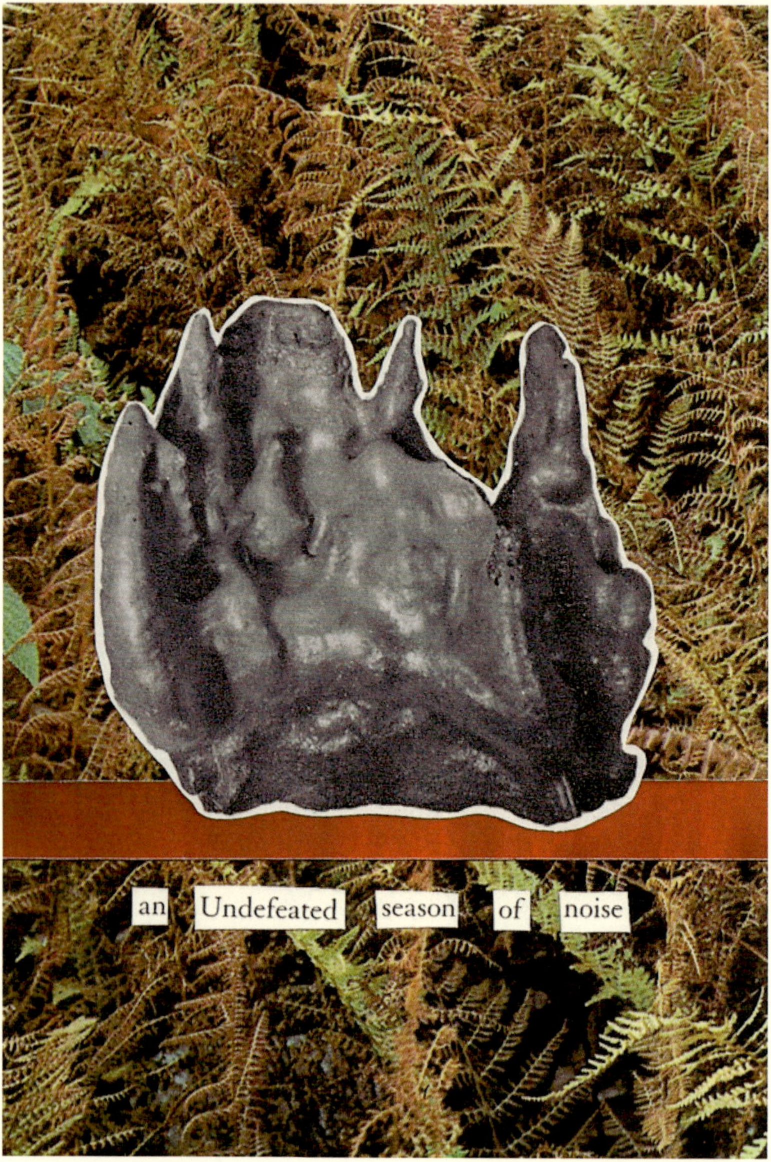
an Undefeated season of noise

DAY 24

Dear Adriene,

Female bears sleep right through birth. You say, *give your little belly a pet*—you say, *smear a little honey across the ribcage*—but visualize for me waking up, unaware of any sign of danger, with sore teats and tiny eyes you can't escape. I've never wanted not to be a mother more than now, half-asleep with heat. Instead, I claim this fusty cave, a lunar flag "waving." You say, *notice how you feel*, and I assure you, I've been trying.

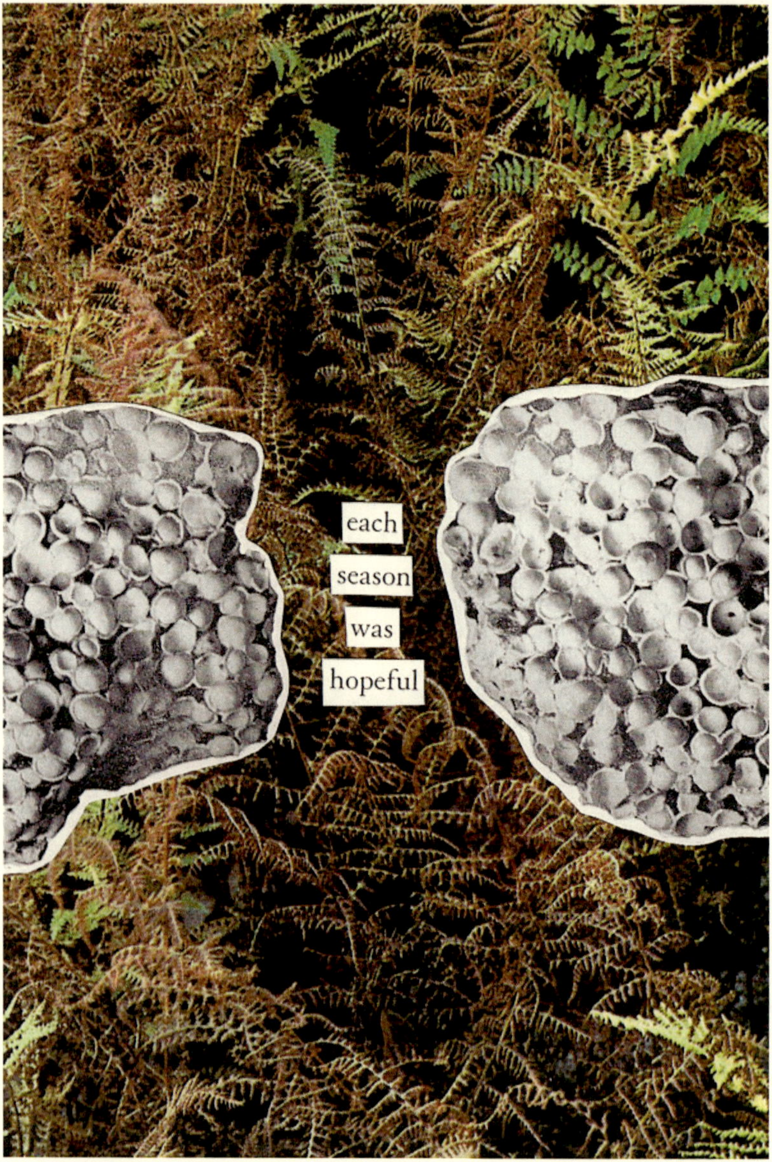
each
season
was
hopeful

DAY 25

Dear Adriene,

The fact sheet says that no one can know when a waterbody named "pond" becomes a waterbody named "lake". The difference is not precise. *Focus on sensation.* My waterline is tree-girt, surrounded by bog laurel and homeless nettles. *Send energy out in all directions*—most importantly through the fruiting bodies of fungus. Let mushrooms gorge on every piece of the evidence we let decay.

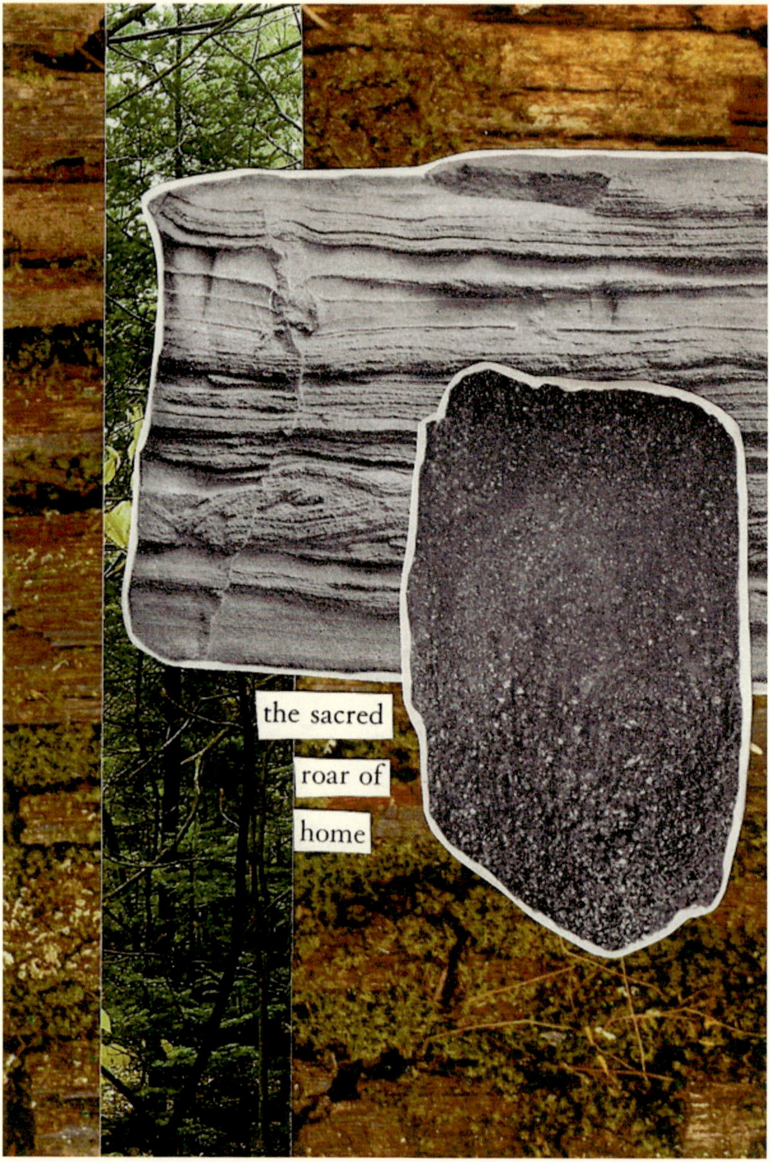
the sacred
roar of
home

DAY 26

Dear Adriene,

I'm sorry, but it was terrifying when you screamed *OH MY GOD, CREAKY FLOOR!* out of nowhere. *The hardest part is over.* Lies leaf-out late—clotted and dirty. I bloom, mad and wild, on the carpeted floor of a cold laundry room. Outside, gray-bearded green & daisies plate the open places. You say, *chase the light,* and I say, add this October to the tens, the hundreds, the millions of Octobers that have gone before it.

DAY 27

Dear Adriene,

What are you waiting for? A better body, straighter teeth, a taste for it, for him to come to me, for someone to just ask, a warmer day, a better bathtub, the check in the mail, the mouse in the kitchen, for someone to say it first, for a second, the bell, the bus, my eyebrows to grow in, for any noticeable release, for two dead beetles in the garden, regrowth after frost, for a bag of diatomaceous earth, some lingering gnats, for dirt to clear nail plate, for the collective good, standing in front of her but not hugging her, for fewer people, less caring, for engine data, propeller theory, an owl to fly out of a tree, for someone to explain what they did to me upon waking from a surgery, for lavender in a plastic bin with my name on it, *permission to do absolutely nothing*, for thunder echoing over a lake, for clouds indistinguishable from smoke, for more blood, for no blood, for your voice older or at the very least sober, for a different way of knowing, knowing the different ways of waiting, the circle inside of a circle, the next chip in my tooth, for my favorite porn clip, for suckers on the tomato plants, cars that sound like rushing water, a way to take back touch, for the squash to turn tan uniformly, for the routine to settle in, for a lie that's good enough to tell myself, the third of any two things I've ever found, for a pair of large pine cones, for a red rotary phone, two matchbooks containing original matches, for twenty-four pages of results, the storm surge, for the strength to say it out loud, for the shapes of poems as poems themselves, for a juicy titbit, lyrical honesty, a matching set of sheds dropped in the same place, for snapping turtle season, for a cold scent, for dirt and purpose, for absorption and collecting, for a formal encounter, confidence in the object from a distance, for the fossilised air of second chances, for water to rush through radiator pipes, for the book that is the notes on the book, for a private place to piss, for the night hunter, for a thaw that hangs around, for stands of maple whips, an antidote to shame, *for just one loving gesture.*

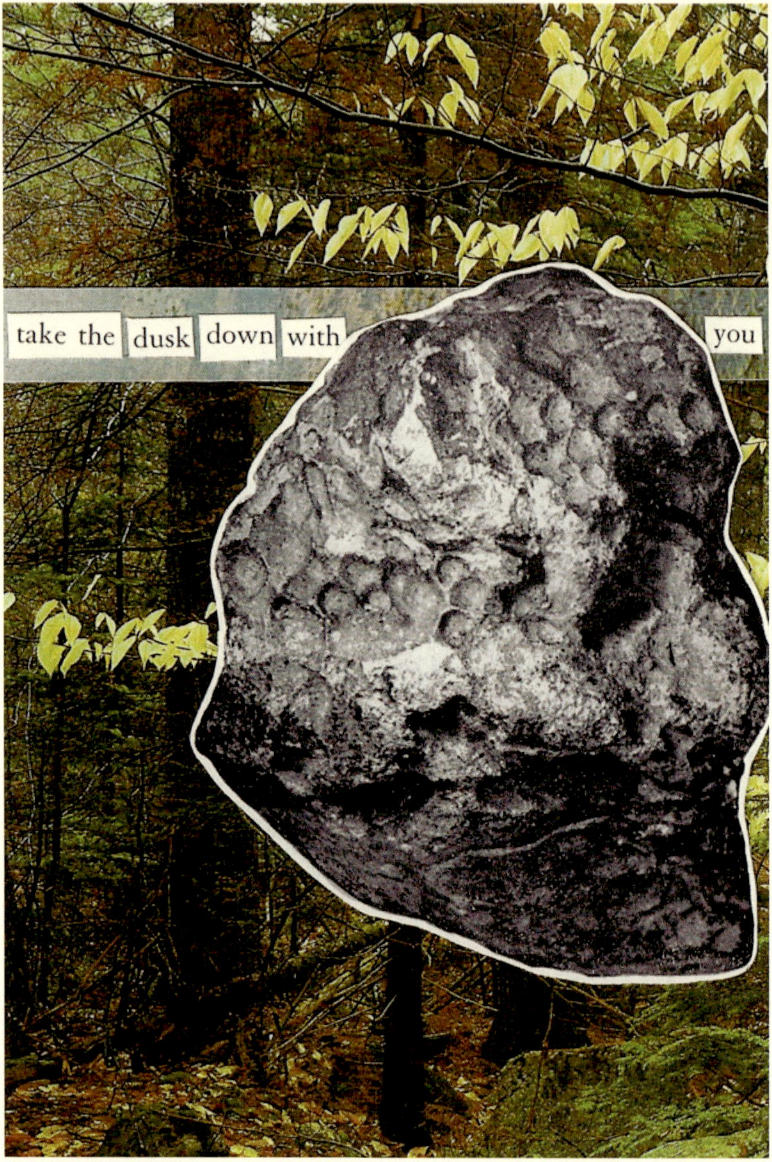
take the dusk down with you

DAY 28

Dear Adriene,

What do the algorithms tell you about me? The continuous coming of people who need you. We are subject to the fewest possible number of rules—like pine duff collecting for years beneath a tall tree. We are spongey, a new breed of grabbers. *You carve out, you tap in, you take responsibility for your balance.* Where first comes one, the next year there are ten, the year after, fully one hundred. *We're just maximizing each moment.* Think of the data they have now, even on you.

DAY 29

Dear Adriene,

Like beasts lying crouched we rise—*from the ground up.* We're not swimming, we're just interacting with water. They said dusk was asking for it, you can tell by what she was wearing. *Let your heel kiss the ground* and dig in. What influence have the months had? How have you been changed? For me, it's like being lost outside at night—every sound a silent scream. I hoist myself into each day, heavy with what it might bring.

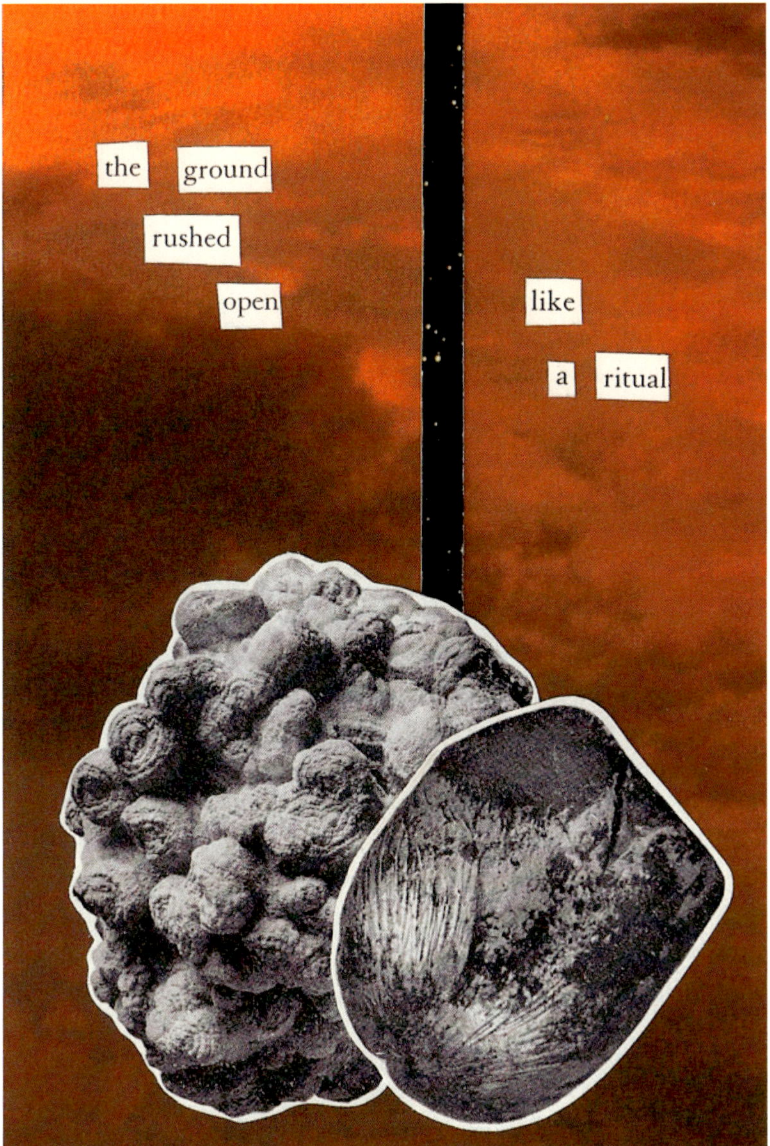
the ground
rushed
open
like
a ritual

DAY 30

Dear Adriene,

Through a computer screen we are two neighboring solitudes. *Take a bird's eye view of yourself.* Is this a mirror or a mimic? At what point does drop become puddle? As usual, all my questions go unanswered but still you chatter warmly. An illusion describes a misinterpretation of a true sensation. *Finish this sentence: I choose* ______________.

NOTES

Some of the poems in this collection use found language inspired by the following sources:

Adriene Mishler's YouTube channel "Yoga with Adriene."

Adirondack Country by William Chapman White, Little, Brown & Co., 1954.

Bleachers by John Grisham.

Collection of objects from Anne LaBastille's cabin as seen in The Adirondack Experience Collections Database.

"Electrostatic forces in wind-pollination—Part 1: Measurement of the electrostatic charge on pollen" by George E. Bowker and Hugh C. Crenshaw (*Atmospheric Environment*, Volume 41, Issue 8, March 2007, p. 1587-1595).

Google search on Rainer Maria Rilke.

"Grain entrapment" entry from Wikipedia.

Index Cards by Moyra Davey.

"Parasocial interaction" entry from Wikipedia.

Part of a found poem by Jane Boxall, read aloud at the 2020 Anne LaBastille Writers Residency.

Personal correspondence from Meg Prichard, 2020.

Quote by Emily Weitzman, spoken aloud after jumping into Twitchell Lake in mid-October with Kate Doyle at the 2020 Anne LaBastille Writers Residency.

"Spotted Lanternfly" entry from National Pest Management Association.

The Complete Book of Boating: Second Edition by Ernest A. Zadig (Prentice Hall, 1976, p. 36).

The Hundreds by Lauren Berlant & Kathleen Stewart.

The Undying by Anne Boyer.

ACKNOWLEDGEMENTS

Some of the poems in this collection have appeared in the following publications and are reproduced with thanks: *Autofocus*, *HAD*, and *Tolka.*

Thank you to the following people and organizations:

Tyler Barton, Meg Prichard, Jenni B. Baker, Libby Modern, Megan Volpert, Amy McDaniel, Adam Robinson, Meghan Phillips, The Hutch, Monica Tojek, Lina Seijo, Dennis Herbert, Sheila Kasperek, Cassie Mannes Murray, Creatives Rebuild New York, The Adirondack Center for Writing, Trish Haverstick and Lemon Street Market, Michael Wheaton and the team at Autofocus, Constance Saltonstall Foundation for the Arts, Jane Boxall, Kate Doyle, Kelsey Francis, Alison Strack, Emily Weitzman, E. Kristin Anderson, Sara Adams, Sarah Nichols, and the poets of *The Poeming.*

Thank you, Adriene, my pandemic friend.

ABOUT THE AUTHOR

Erin Dorney is the author of *I Am Not Famous Anymore: Poems After Shia LaBeouf*; *Grating, Darling, Full of Dirt*; *The Usual Arteries*; *Yes I Am Human I Know You Were Wondering*; and many zines. Her writing has appeared in *DIAGRAM, Tolka, Passages North, Juked, Bone Bouquet,* and *HAD*, among other publications. Her literary artwork and installations have been featured at the Center for Maine Contemporary Art, Hennepin Theatre Trust, the Minnesota Center for Book Arts, and Susquehanna Art Museum. Erin has been awarded residencies at Saltonstall, Soaring Gardens, Hewnoaks, Tofte Lake Center, Anne LaBastille Memorial Writers Residency, and Spruceton Inn. She is the co-founder of Fear No Lit and lives in New York.

[a]

— also from Autofocus Books —

Duplex — Mike Nagel

XO — Sara Rauch

Until It Feels Right — Emily Costa

Cleave — Holly Pelesky

Nextdoor in Colonialtown — Ryan Rivas

Too Much Tongue — Adrienne Marie Barrios & Leigh Chadwick

Picture Window — Danny Caine

the nature machine! — Tyler Gillespie

A Kind of In-Between — Aaron Burch

How to Write a Novel: An Anthology of 20 Craft Essays About Writing, None of Which Ever Mention Writing — ed. Aaron Burch

Hiraeth — Mistie Watkins

That Spell — Tate N. Oquendo

My Modest Blindness — Russell Brakefield

A Calendar Is A Snakeskin — Kristine Langley Mahler

Culdesac — Mike Nagel

Razed by TV Sets — Jason McCall

In the Away Time — Kristen E. Nelson

The Body Is A Temporary Gathering Place — Andrew Bertaina

Daughterhood — Emily Adrian

Leave: A Postpartum Account — Shayne Terry